A Brand Strategist's Note

A FEW THINGS COMPANY

/

Copyright © 2018 written and illustrated by Sophia Ahn
Published by A Few Things Company. Book design by Sophia Ahn.
All rights reserved. No part of this book may be reproduced in any form
without written permission from the publisher.

Title: A Brand Strategist's Note | Author: Sophia Ahn
ISBN-13: 978-1983859380 | ISBN-10: 1983859389
Printed in the United States of America. Manufacture by CreateSpace.
Distributed by Amazon.

www.afewthingscompany.com

For brand thinkers

Sophia Ahn is a brand strategist consulting multinational corporates and not-for-profit organizations including schools and foundations both in the United States and Korea. With a master's degree from Carnegie Mellon University and a knack for thriving in culturally diverse business settings, Sophia hopes to discover creative solutions to brand related problems and generate positive energy for people around her.

sophia@afewthingscompany.com

/

Brand is ubiquitous and easily talked about, but in order for the brand to come out and be communicated, people behind it who develop and manage the brand are going through some heavy thinking and tricky challenges. Branding is hard. There's no right answer, no one solution, no better approach or no exact method. Fighting with the quite intangible concepts and trying to create a certainty out of it, brand strategists and mangers often get locked in a complexity of the branding processes.

This book does not give specific directions or tips for branding, but it rather leaves the readers with further questions on certain topics. Hope this can be a gateway for beginners of brand & communications leading to deeper investigations, and maybe a nudge for brand professionals to refresh and think back on the basics of branding.

January 2018
Sophia Ahn

Where do I begin...?

Tom Peters

American business consultant, author, speaker, and management guru.
<In Search of Excellence> <The Circle of Innovation> etc.
www.tompeters.com

> When one has an identity, life gets a whole lot simpler. The problem is an identity that matters is insanely hard to inculcate. Insanely hard to maintain.

- Tom Peters

Putting oneself in a few and simple words is only possible after profound contemplation and the deep understanding of the self. Knowing oneself, that's the beginning of it.

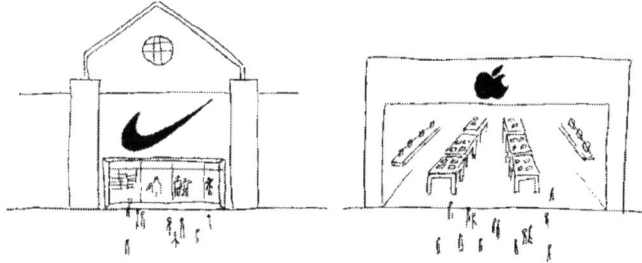

Visual identity – the logos and symbols – plays an important role to secure the brand visibility, but it doesn't entirely stand for the brand identity.

You can say advertisements are what
eventually and directly reach to the people,
but it's only a part of the brand strategy.

05

David Aaker

American author, brand and marketing guru, professor, and business consultant.
Creator of the Aaker Model™
<Managing Brand Equity> <Brand Leadership> <Brand Portfolio Strategy> etc.

> Advertising's role in the process of building and communicating the meaning of a brand is as a part within a larger whole.

- David Aaker

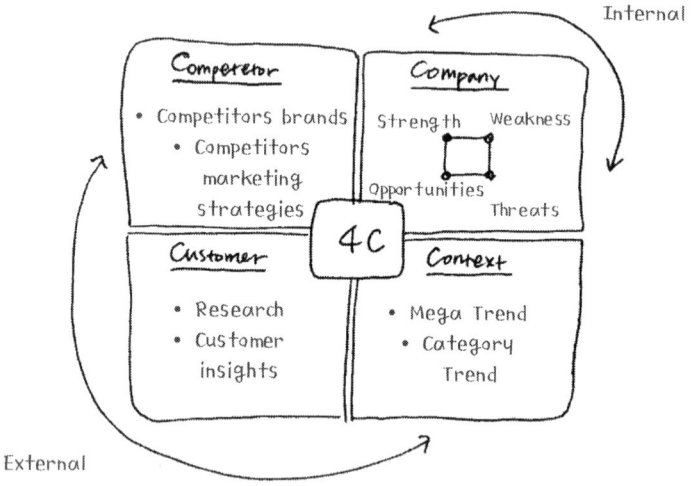

4C analysis, SWOT analysis, or whatever you call it — analyze the internal and external factors meticulously and exhaustively.

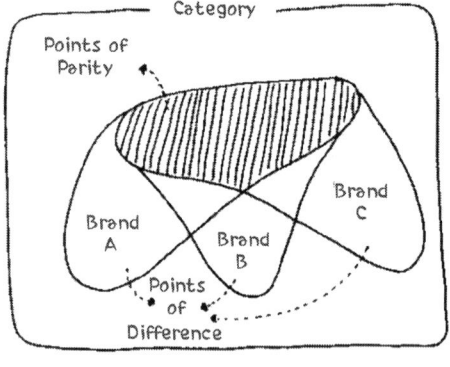

Your brand's remarkableness won't come from the points of parity. Discover the points of difference of your brand.

08

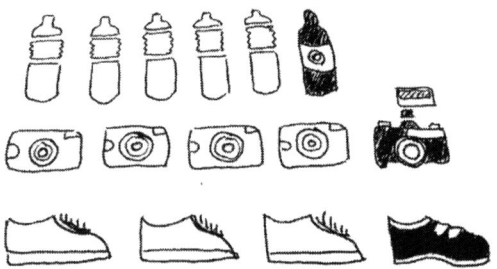

* From the book <Different> by Youngme Moon

You can't truly differentiate your brand without thinking outside the box and see the world with a new point of view.

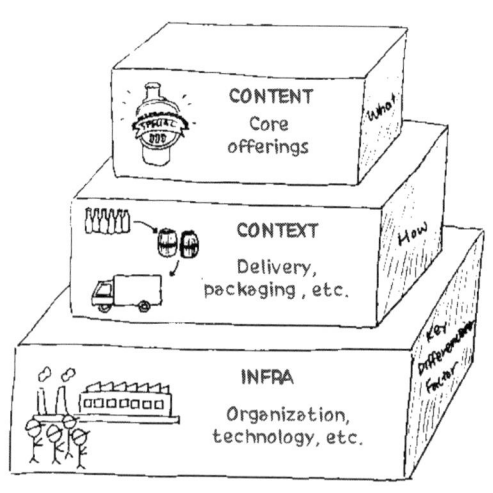

Differentiating factors can be found in infra, context, and contents.

10

Howard Gardner

American developmental psychologist, author, professor.
<Frames of Mind> <Multiple Intelligences Around the World>
<Leading Minds> etc.

> Discover your difference, the asynchrony with which you have been blessed or cursed, and make the most of it.

- Howard Gardner

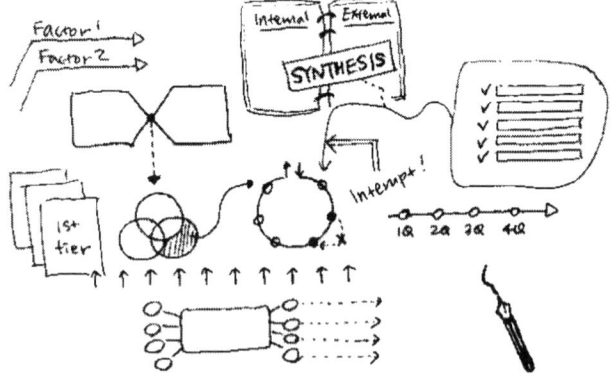

Developing brand strategy requires
visualization of the intangibles and
effective communication of those.

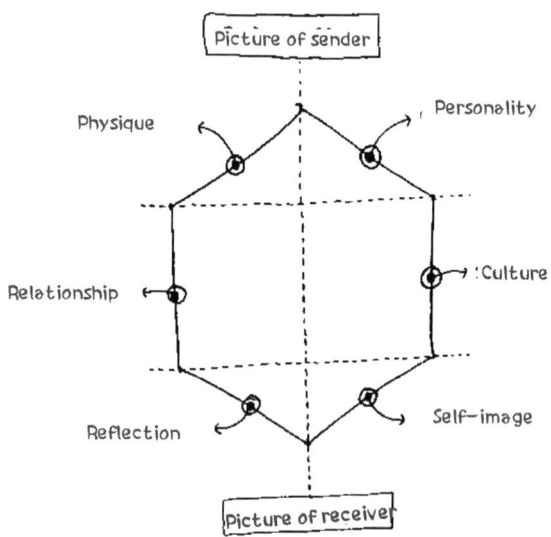

* Jean-Noël Kapferer's Brand Prism

There's no single right format to diagnose the brand identity. Use a framework that works best for your brand.

Brand. Balance.

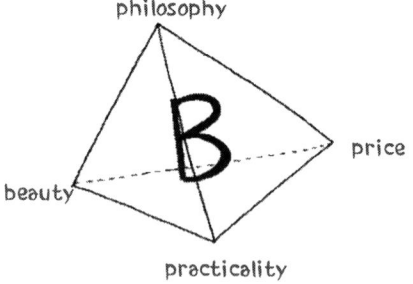

* Brand Identity of Magazine B

There's no single right format to express the brand identity. Use a diagram that works best for your brand.

Research/Patterns/insights   →   !

Ideas are never born instantaneously.
Only arduous thinking journey bears good ideas.

Concepts should be one and simple.
Perhaps in three words or a short sentence.
No brand strategy would be successful
with a concept that's complex.

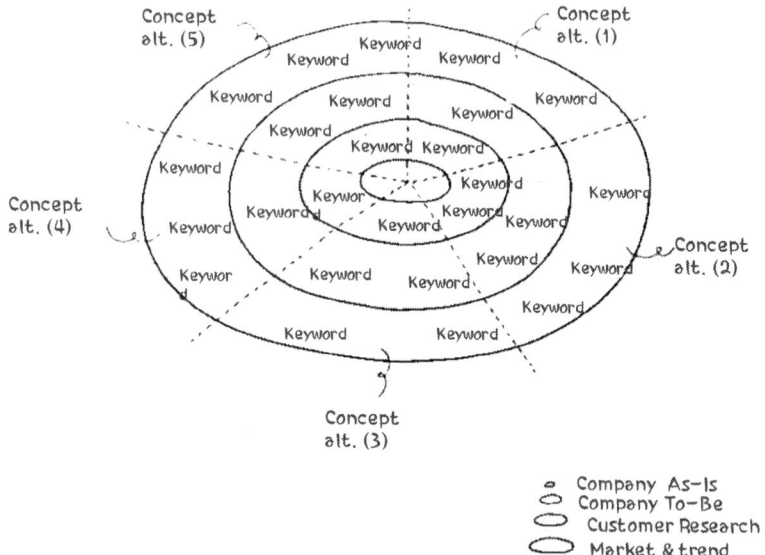

Scattering, dividing, and combining the keywords is a process of developing concepts.

Malcolm Gladwell

Canadian journalist, author, and speaker.
<Blink> <Outliers> <The Tipping Point> etc.

"

Being able to act intelligently and instinctively
in the moment is possible only after a long and
rigorous of education and experience.

"

- Malcolm Gladwell

As the brands get mature, their logos tend to be more simplified. Less to talk out loud.

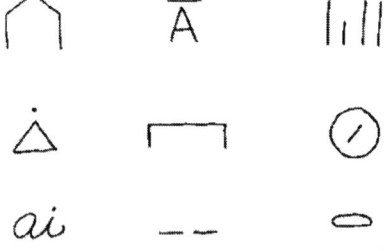

Not because the brand got mature,
sometime simplicity act as a strategic core.
Know what stage of life your brand is at
and if your brand identity pursues
simplicity in its philosophy.

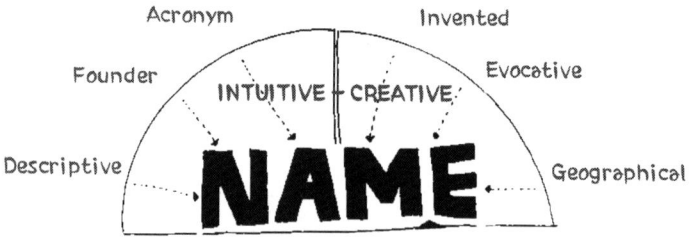

Naming does not magically appear from out of nowhere, but it is born after examination of various possibilities.

There are issues around the brand all the time. Brand renewal is not always the answer.

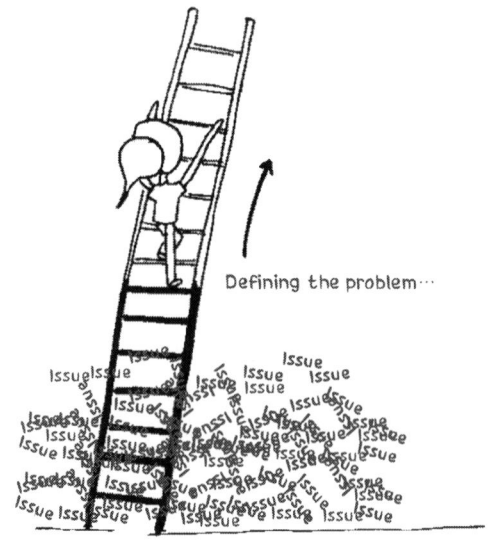

Extending target market?
New competition?
Brand rejuvenation needed?
Defining the problem solves the problem
half way through.

Denise Lee Yohn

Brand strategist, author, speaker.
<What Great Brands Do> <Scale Up Your Brand Workbook> <Fusion> etc.

> Brands need to be informed by customers but led by their brand.

- Denise Lee Yohn

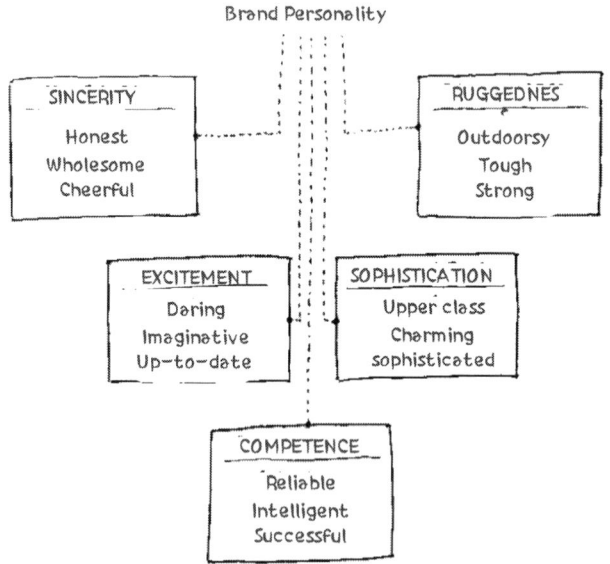

* Brand personality framework by David Aaker

People tend to see brands as human. Use the adjective in brand personality framework and think about what kind of person your brand could be.

Having one's own unique color can be a huge advantage. Try to be a brand that can be easily recognized.

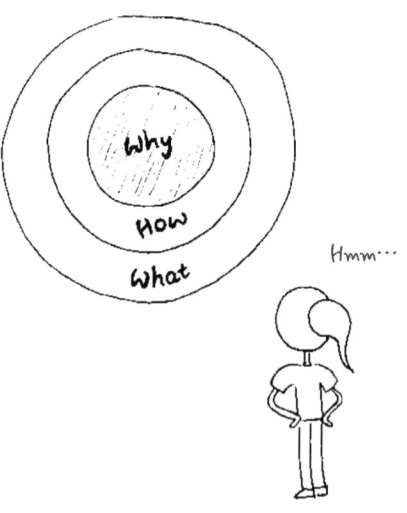

* Golden Circle by Simon Sinek

'People don't buy what you do.
They buy why you do it.'
Take a moment and contemplate on your why.

Sasha Strauss

Brand strategist at American brand consulting firm
'Innovation protocol'

> Don't communicate until you know exactly who you are and why you matter. Only then are you ready to share your message with the world.

- *Sasha Strauss*

After brand strategy is set, a large number of people would have to use and practice the brand in various ways. List up do's and don'ts for your brand and let the people apply as the guideline says.

Damaging your brand reputation can be a fatal loss. Building a brand reputation takes a long time, but losing it happens at one moment.

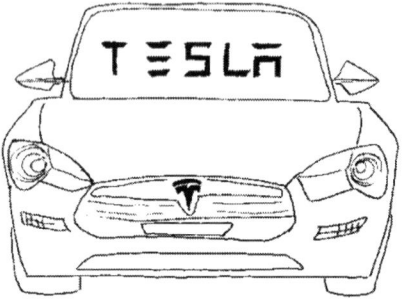

Dream big.
Push the boundaries.
Become a game changer.

WARBY PARKER
eyewear

UBER

Disruptive brands achieve things
considered to be unachievable.

Adam Grant

Organizational psychologist, professor, author.
<Originals> <Give and Take> etc.

> The greatest shapers don't stop at introducing originality into the world. They create cultures that unleash originality in others.

- Adam Grant

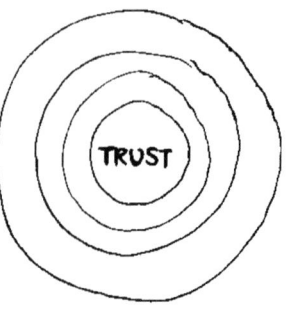

Strategy without practice is useless.

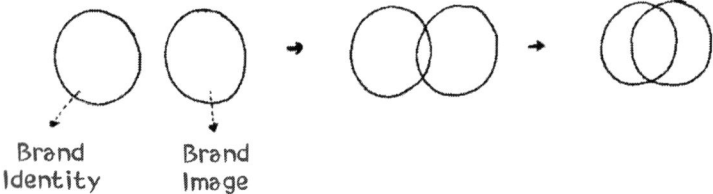

Brand Identity   Brand Image

Brand management is about reducing the gap between brand identity and brand image. It is multi dimensional and total directional.

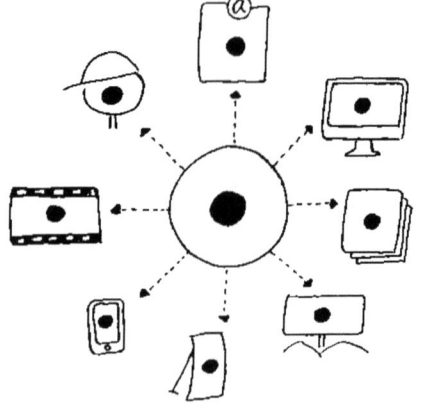

Consistency is key for effective communication.

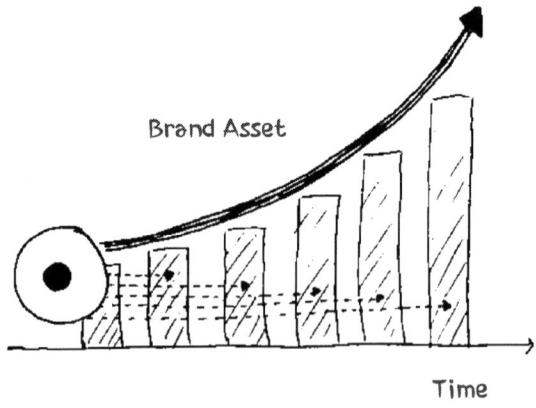

Continuity is key for efficient communication.

* Illustration: Modern Love, New Yorker

Consuming the brand means not just buying a product or service, but it means the customer accepts the brand's philosophy and make the philosophy of her own.

Dan Ariely

Professor of Psychology and Behavioral Economics, author.
<Predictably Irrational> <The Upside of Irrationality> etc.

> Brands communicate in two directions: they help us tell other people something about ourselves, but they also help us form ideas about who we are.

- Dan Ariely

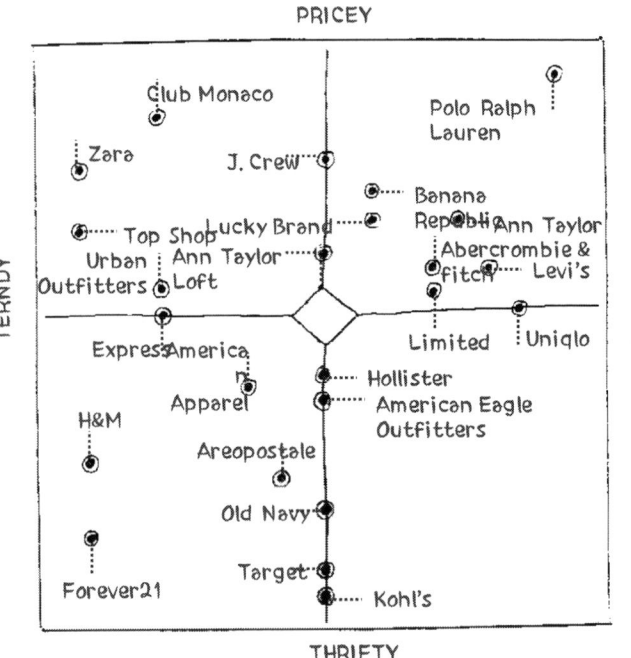

* Fashion brands positioning map by Gap

Why you choose Forever21 over H&M;
Why you buy your boy friend's sweater
from J. Crew, not from Banana republic.
Why your mom prefers Target over Kohl's.
How people select one brand over another
when both brands provides almost the same
functional attributes lies on the emotional
values.

Nancy King

Head of Brand, Airbnb

"

When a company is growing as fast and organically as us, you can assume that it's going to grow like that forever. But there are companies like Expedia or Priceline that are spending five times as much trying to go after the same people, trying to move into our space. How do we win against them over time? New startups are also coming in, trying to replicate our business model. How do we win against that? Historically there was a belief in Silicon Valley that technological IP made you win. You have something that nobody else can build. You patent it. But Airbnb doesn't have that. In an environment where people can copy what we have, what prevents people from choosing those other companies over us?

"

- Nancy King

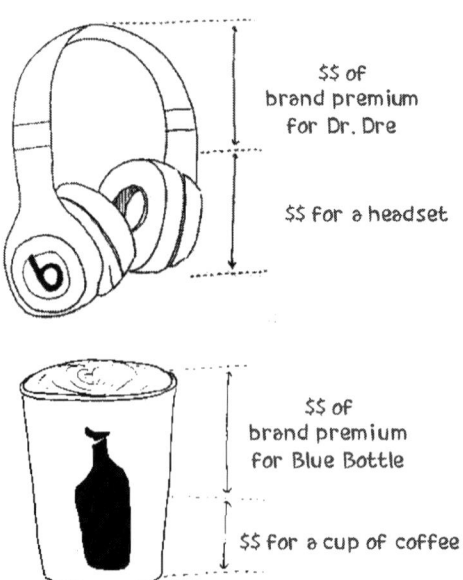

People willingly pay a brand premium for the brands they love.

Ross Buck

Professor of Communication and Psychology at University of Connecticut

> Motivation and emotion are two sides of the same coin.

- Ross Buck

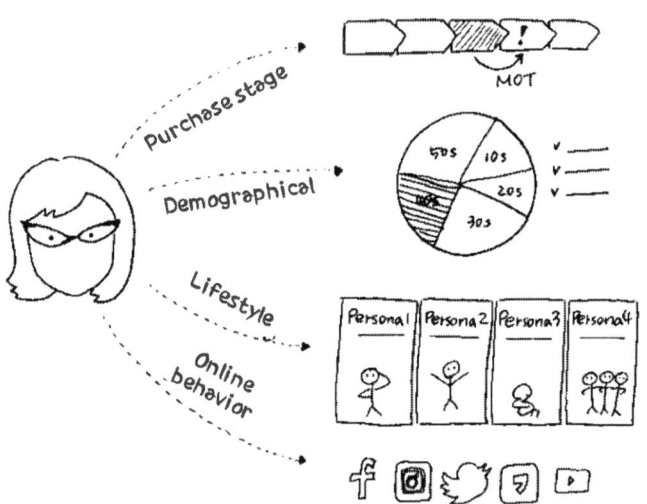

There are many ways to look at the customers. Determine in what base you will analyze them first.

$$\text{Brand Power} = \frac{\text{Brand Value}}{\text{Distance between the Brand and the customers}}$$

Brand power gets bigger as it gets closer to the customers.

What you say is what I say...

Brand is a relationship.

Create brand fandom.
Let them be your fan, form a community, send you gifts, participate in new product planning, tattoo your logo, etc.
Your brand will become stronger.

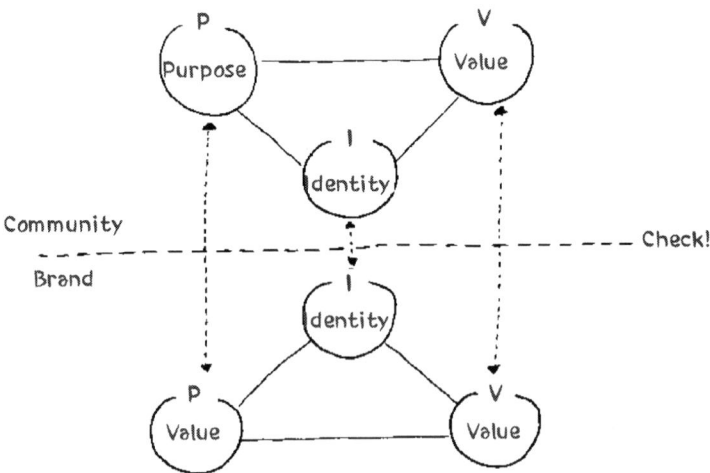

* Community and PVI, <Marketing for Competitiveness> by Philip Kotler

Brand's purpose, values, and the identity should align with the customer community's purpose, values, and the identity.

Seth Godin

Blogger, author, entrepreneur, agent of change.
<Permission Marketing> <Purple Cow> <All Marketers Are Liars> 등

"

They're building an asset that has nothing to do with brand and everything to do with their relationship with you.

"

- Seth Godin

Balance between the strategy and the creative is critical.

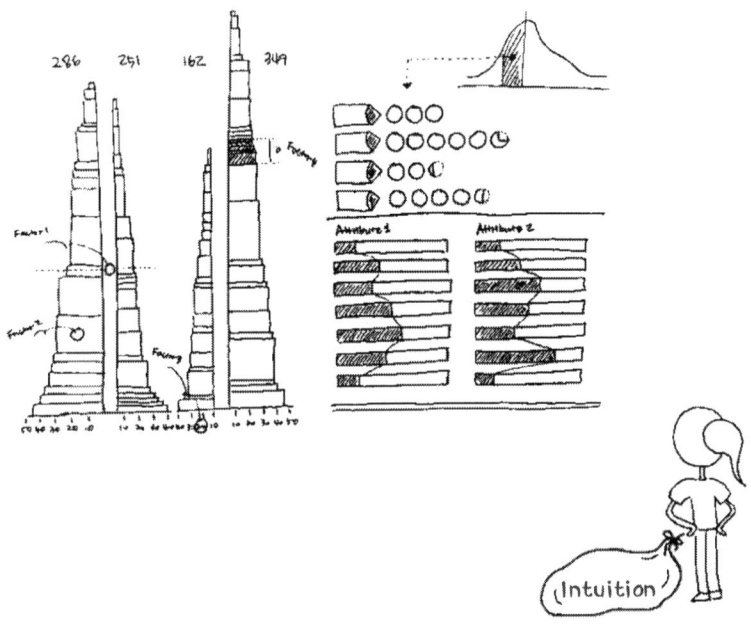

Be flexible and find a harmony somewhere between the data and the intuition.

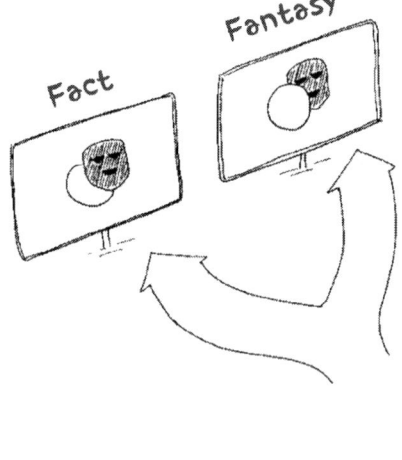

Be flexible and find a harmony somewhere between the facts and the fantasies.

Various reframing of talking about a tree

A direct way of talking about something can be less attractive. What could be a smart and meaningful 'reframing' of talking about your brand?

Steve Jobs

American entrepreneur, founder of Apple

> Sell dreams, not products.
> If you help your customers reach their dreams,
> you'll win them over.

— *Steve Jobs*

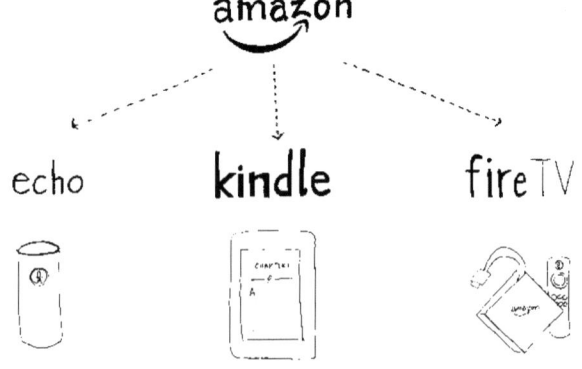

Extend the brand only in alignment with the existing brand values.

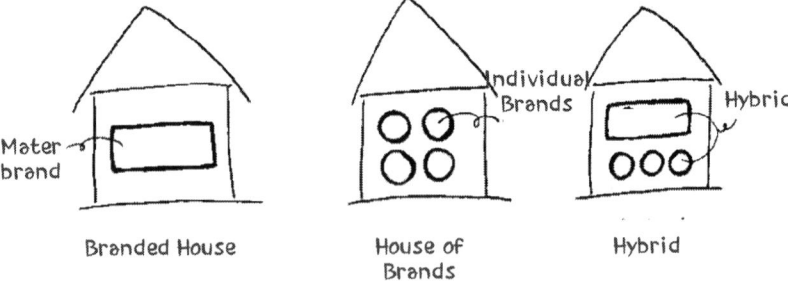

Organize multiple brands in structure.

| Master brand |
| Sub brand |

Sub brand by Master brand

Master brand | Sub brand

Review the right type of brand endorsement for your brands portfolio.

You can't teach your employees a brand. They need to understand and experience the brand themselves, and foster an advocate mind of their own.

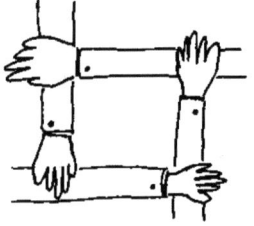

Sometimes an attitude is more important than a perspective for brand building.

Jim Collins

Business consultant, author
<Good to Great> <Built to Last and How the Mighty Fall> etc.
www.jimcollins.com

> Great vision without great people is irrelevant.

— *Jim Collins*

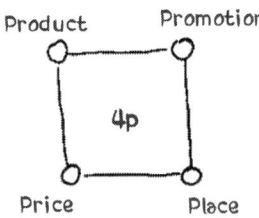
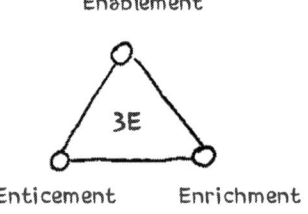

* 3E concept from a book <Brand Admiration> by C. Whan Park, Deborah J. MacInnis, Andreas B. Eisingerich, Allen M. Weiss

Sometimes framework determines quality of the thinking. Consider new marketing mix of 3E based on what values customers look for in brands.
Be admired.

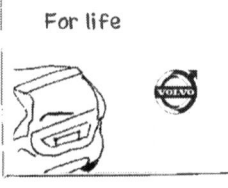

Slogan is a statement for positioning. Every brand is responsible for their statements. Slogan itself does not make sense unless the other marketing activities are coherent to what the brand means to say.

Communication slogan works better when it's no more than one and strong, but the message can be varied – as far as the core of the brand message is maintained.

When leveraging your brand through influencers, spreading the message as wide as you could is good, but cultivating true organic customers is better.

Hold on to your belief, stick to the knitting when necessary, and avoid brand dilution.

Brand equity is the final destination of the brand's life.

Iconic brands have courage and confidence.
Learn from them.

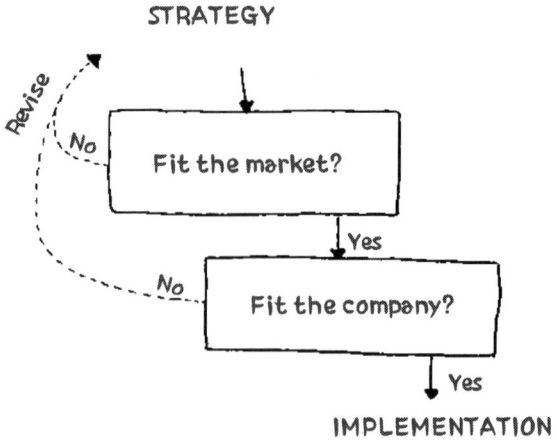

Strategies that worked for some iconic brands can look good and plausible, but it doesn't make sense if it doesn't fit your company. Revise and make it work for your brand.

69

Xenophon

Greek philosopher, historian, soldier, mercenary, and student of Socrates.
<Memories of Socrates>

> If someone knows what is good, he will do what is good, because he will aim for what is good.

- Xenophon

Made in the USA
San Bernardino, CA
16 February 2018